101 Gourmet

Cupcakes

IN 10 MINUTES

Text © 2009 by Wendy L. Paul
Photographs © 2009 by Marielle Hayes

ISBN: 978-1-59955-259-0

Published by CFI, an imprint of Cedar Fort, Inc., 2373 W. 700 S., Springville, UT 84663
Distributed by Cedar Fort, Inc., www.cedarfort.com

LIBRARY OF CONGRESS CATALOGING-IN-PUBLICATION DATA

Paul, Wendy.
  101 gourmet cupcakes in 10 minutes / Wendy Paul.
    p. cm.
  ISBN 978-1-59955-259-0 (acid-free paper)
  1. Cupcakes. I. Title. II. Title: One hundred one gourmet cupcakes in ten
minutes. III. Title: One hundred and one gourmet cupcakes in ten minutes.

  TX771.P377 2009
  641.8'653--dc22

  2009006650

Cover and page design by Angela D. Olsen
Cover design © 2009 by Lyle Mortimer
Edited and typeset by Kimiko M. Hammari
Printed in China

10 9 8 7 6 5 4 3 2 1

Printed on acid-free paper

101 Gourmet Cupcakes

IN 10 MINUTES

WENDY PAUL
CFI
SPRINGVILLE, UTAH

For my mother, grandmothers, and mother-in-law.
Each of you have inspired me to bake with creativity,
given me encouragement, and taught me
everything I know. Thank you.

Contents

Small Cakes with Big Ideas

I *have always loved* spending time in the kitchen, creating new and delicious recipes. Many friends and family members call me and ask for recipes, so I decided to write them down and make a cookbook. Cupcakes are a perfect dessert, party theme, gift, get-well favor, or "just because I love you" treat. So my idea is thinking outside the box. Why not make a special cupcake with the convenience of using a cake mix? I know what you're thinking: "Will it taste homemade?" You bet!

By using the recipes and time-saving ideas in this book, your cupcakes will look and taste like you slaved away the entire afternoon creating these little masterpieces. Go ahead and dust your face with a little flour to get the recognition you deserve. I won't say a word. Your family and friends will thank you for the wonderful creation you have hand made and home baked. Enjoy the cupcake walk!

—Wendy L. Paul

Tips for Success

Most cupcake recipes average closer to 18 cupcakes rather than 24 when baked. Be prepared. When using fillers such as candy and cookies, the batter will make closer to 24 cupcakes.

When making the chocolate ganache, if the chocolate hasn't melted after putting the hot cream over it, place it in the microwave and cook on medium heat for 30 seconds. Stir again until chocolate is smooth.

If you desire to make several kinds of cupcakes with one cake mix, here's the trick: Make batter without adding flavoring. Separate batter into equal portions—let's say three—and then divide other ingredient amounts by $1/3$. For example, chocolate almond, chocolate zucchini, and chocolate cream would all work well because they have a similar batter base.

Shaped cupcake tins are available in round, heart, star, and square. You can usually find them in the cake decorating aisle at your local grocery store. Specialized tins are a great way to mix things up without a lot of extra cost.

Don't be afraid to mix and match frostings with different cake bases. Make the cake that your family will enjoy!

Cupcakes with cream frosting or filling will need to be refrigerated after baking and being frosted. They can last up to one week covered in the refrigerator. (I have yet to have had that happen—at my house, they're eaten within days!)

If you don't have a wire rack for cooling the cupcakes, don't fret. Tip the cupcakes on their side to rest so that air flows freely around the bottom. That way, they won't sweat while cooling.

To get your cupcakes a uniform size, use a cookie scoop that measures ¼ cup. This is a perfect way to get equal round tops every time.

A small, uneven spatula not only makes frosting cakes easier, but can also aid you in removing cupcakes from the pan. Simply slide the spatula between the paper liner and the pan, and carefully lift.

If a recipe calls for butter, please do not skimp and use margarine. Not only is butter in the name, but you *will* be caught! Butter adds the right flavor!

Don't run out of frosting. For 12 cupcakes you will need 1 cup frosting. For 24 cupcakes you will need 2 cups, and so on. If you plan to be more generous and pile the frosting high, add an additional cup for every 12 cupcakes.

If you are looking to trim a little fat from some recipes, you can easily substitute regular cream cheese with a reduced-fat cream cheese. But I would much rather have the real thing and less of it, than more of a low-fat version.

Use dry cake mixes in the recipes unless otherwise specified.

Small plastic sandwich bags are a perfect way to frost easily and mess-free. Scoop frosting inside the bag and squeeze all the air out. Then seal. Cut a small hole with your scissors at one bottom end of the bag. Carefully apply pressure to the bag starting at the top, aiming at the cupcake to frost. Make sure you take a test run so you are confident.

Fabulous & Fruity

Banana Cream Pie
Banana Foster
Banana Streusel
Best Ever Apple
Key Lime Pie
Lemon Blueberry
Lemon Cream
Orange Creamsicle
Orange Poppy Seed
Peach Cobbler
Pear Upside Down

Piña Colada
Pineapple Upside Down
Pink Lemonade
Sour Cream Blueberry
Strawberry Cheesecake
Strawberry Shortcake
Tutti Frutti
Vanilla Pudding Poppy Seed
White Chocolate Strawberry
Yogurt Parfait

Banana Cream Pie

with Whipped Cream

Banana Cream Pie

My mother-in-law makes the best banana cream pie. I have taken her twist to the ever-popular dessert and made it into a cupcake. Wow! Now this is a good cupcake!

1 box yellow cake mix

2 eggs

1 cup half and half

1 tsp. lemon extract

1 package (4-oz.) instant banana cream pudding mix

1 recipe whipped cream

sliced bananas for garnish

Mix together cake mix, eggs, half and half, lemon extract, and pudding mix (powder only).

Pour batter into paper liners and fill ¾ full.

Bake at 350 degrees for 18–20 minutes or until cake springs back when lightly touched. Remove from pan and allow cupcakes to cool on a wire rack.

Top with whipped cream and sliced bananas to garnish.

Frosting Suggestions

Whipped Cream

Banana Foster

I found a nonalcoholic version of banana foster last summer, and my family loves it every time I make it for dessert. This over-the-top creation tastes like it takes forever to make, but in reality it takes no time at all!

1 box white cake mix

2 eggs

¼ cup butter, melted

½ cup milk

1 tsp. artificial rum flavoring

1 small jar of caramel sauce

bananas for garnish

1 recipe whipped cream

Mix together cake mix, eggs, butter, milk, and rum flavoring.

Bake at 350 degrees for 15–18 minutes or until cake springs back when lightly touched. Remove from oven and allow to cool slightly.

Unwrap cupcakes carefully (they will be hot) and drizzle a generous amount of caramel sauce over the tops. Place a dollop of whipped cream and sliced bananas on top of the caramel sauce to garnish.

Frosting Suggestions

Whipped Cream

Banana Streusel

My aunt made a banana cake for my mom and dad during a visit to California. I heard only raves about how delicious and moist it was. Serving this cake is now a tradition among my immediate family members. When I told my mom about this idea for an easy cupcake cookbook, she said I would have to include this recipe, only slightly modified for cupcakes.

- 1 box yellow cake mix, ½ cup reserved for topping
- 3 eggs
- 1 cup half and half
- 1 tsp. vanilla extract
- 4 Tbsp. butter, melted
- 3 ripe bananas, peeled and mashed
- 3 Tbsp. butter
- ½ tsp. cinnamon

Mix together cake mix, eggs, half and half, vanilla, and melted butter until smooth. Fold mashed bananas into batter, and fill the paper liners ¾ full.

In a small bowl, add ½ cup dry cake mix, butter, and cinnamon. Combine with a fork to make crumbs. Evenly sprinkle the crumb mixture on top of all the unbaked cupcakes.

Bake at 350 degrees for 15–18 minutes or until slightly golden brown. Do not overbake—this causes a dry cupcake. Remove from oven and allow to cool slightly before serving with ice cream on the side, or cool completely and frost.

Frosting Suggestions

Vanilla Buttercream · Cream Cheese

Best Ever Apple
with Cream Cheese Frosting

Best Ever Apple

I saw the best recipe for an apple cake on a cooking program years ago. It was loaded with saturated fat and sugar, which I try not to serve my family. I reinvented this cake and made it better tasting and better for you. Now it's a cupcake too!

1 box spice cake mix
2 eggs
2 tsp. vanilla extract
1 tsp. cinnamon
½ cup oil
2 Granny Smith apples cut into ½" pieces, skins on

Mix together cake mix, eggs, vanilla, cinnamon, and oil. Batter will be thick.

Add apples and beat for 2–3 minutes on medium speed. Batter will thin out somewhat. Pour batter into paper liners and fill ¾ full.

Bake at 350 degrees for 18–20 minutes or until cake springs back when lightly touched. Remove from oven and cool completely on a wire rack. Frost once cooled.

Frosting Suggestions
Caramel Cream · Cream Cheese

Key Lime Pie
with Whipped Cream

Key Lime Pie

*Key lime pie is the first official dessert my daughter Addie ever tasted. Her Pappy
fed it to her without me knowing. At first, her mouth puckered
and her eyes watered, but then she asked for more!*

- 1 box white cake mix
- 3 eggs
- 1 cup half and half
- 6 Tbsp. key lime juice
- 1 can sweetened condensed milk
- 1 recipe whipped cream
- 4 Tbsp. grated lime peel (about 3 limes) for garnish

Mix together cake mix, eggs, half and half, and 3 tablespoons key lime juice. Pour 1–2 tablespoons batter into each paper liner. In a separate bowl, mix sweetened condensed milk and the rest of the lime juice. Evenly divide lime milk into batter-filled cups. Top with remaining batter and fill ¾ full.

Bake at 350 degrees for 15–18 minutes or until cake springs back when touched lightly. Remove from oven and cool completely on a wire rack.

Frost with whipped cream and garnish with grated lime peel.

Frosting Suggestions

Whipped Cream

Lemon Blueberry

These two flavors complement each other so well. This cupcake has such a fresh taste and is so tasty for spring and summer. You can also substitute frozen berries for fresh.

1 box lemon cake mix

1 tsp. lemon extract

3 eggs

1 cup milk

1 can blueberry pie filling

powdered sugar to garnish

1 recipe whipped cream

Mix together cake mix, lemon extract, eggs, and milk. Beat at medium speed until light and fluffy.

Pour 2 tablespoons cake batter into each paper liner. Add 2 tablespoons pie filling on top. Add remaining cake batter, dividing evenly among all the cupcakes.

Bake at 350 degrees for 15–18 minutes or until top is lightly golden brown. Remove from oven and cool on a wire rack.

Dust with powdered sugar and top with remaining pie filling and whipped cream.

Frosting Suggestions

Whipped Cream

Lemon Cream

with Whipped Cream

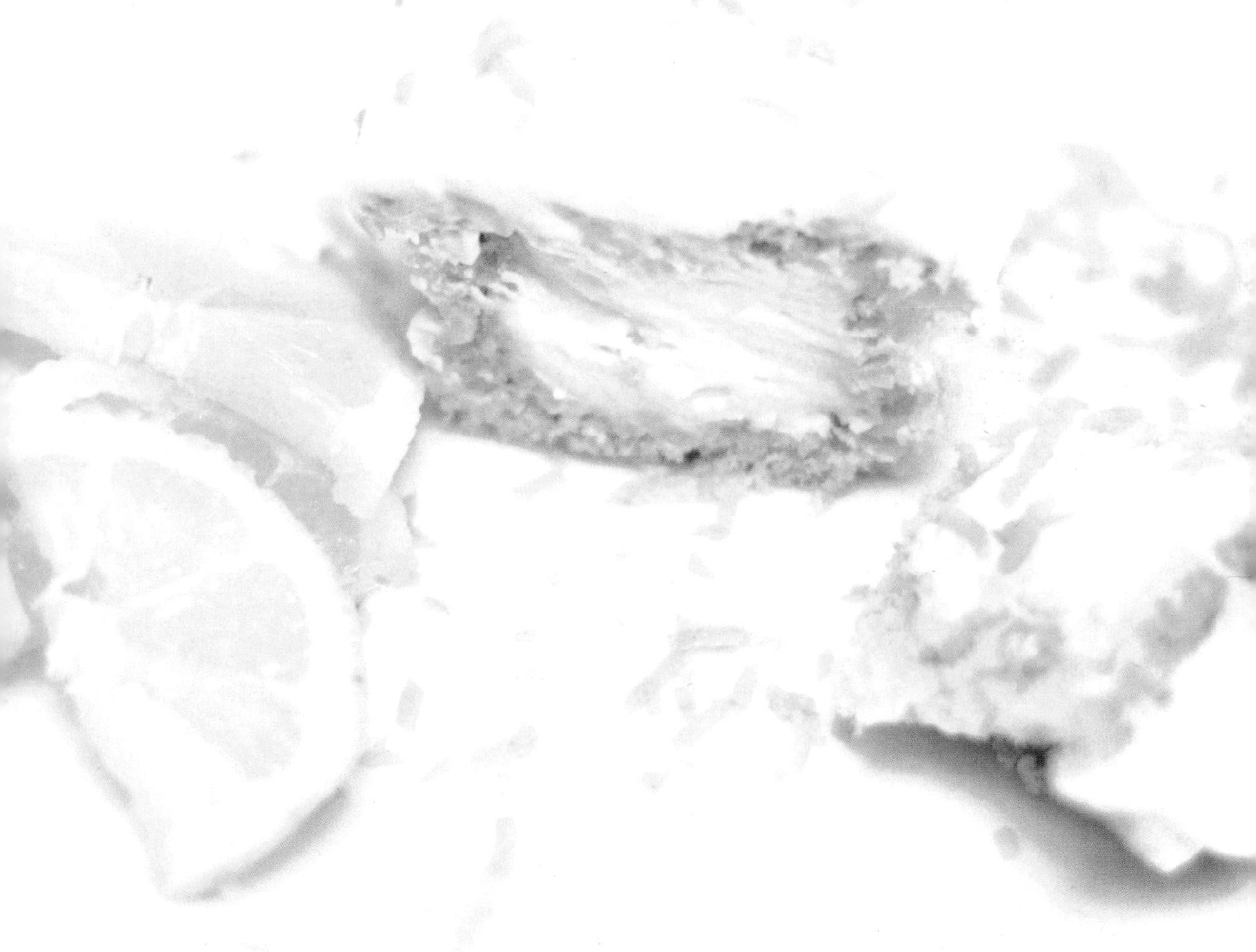

Lemon Cream

The smell of lemons refreshes you and can brighten any gloomy day.
The taste is even better!

1 box lemon cake mix

2 eggs

1 cup sour cream

1 package (8-oz.) cream cheese, softened

2 Tbsp. grated lemon zest

1 recipe whipped cream

1 tsp. lemon extract

½ cup crushed lemon drop candy

Mix together cake mix, eggs, sour cream, and cream cheese until smooth and creamy. Add grated lemon zest and combine. Fill paper liners ¾ full.

Bake at 350 degrees for 15–18 minutes or until cake springs back when lightly touched. Remove and cool cupcakes on a wire rack.

Add lemon extract to whipped cream and combine well. Top cooled cupcakes with lemon whipped cream and sprinkle with crushed lemon candy for garnish.

Frosting Suggestions
Lemon Whipped Cream

Orange Creamsicle

On a hot summer day, nothing tastes better than a cold creamsicle.
This cupcake, especially when served cold, is a perfect treat!

- 1 box yellow cake mix
- 2 eggs
- 1 cup milk
- 2–3 drops yellow food coloring
- 1–2 drops red food coloring
- ⅓ cup orange juice concentrate
- 1 recipe whipped cream

Mix together cake mix, eggs, and milk. Drop enough yellow and red food coloring to make a good orange colored batter. Pour batter into paper liners and fill ¾ full.

Bake at 350 degrees for 15–18 minutes or until cake springs back when lightly touched. Remove from oven and place on a wire rack until cooled.

Once the cupcakes are cool, cut out the top, set aside, and make a place for the filling, leaving the walls and bottom of the cupcake strong enough to support the filling.

In a separate bowl, fold ⅓ cup orange juice concentrate into whipped cream. Spoon the filling into the hole and top with set aside portion of cupcake to seal the filling. Top with desired frosting or a dollop of any leftover filling mixture.

Frosting Suggestions

Cream Cheese • Vanilla Buttercream • Whipped Cream

Orange Poppy Seed

with Cream Cheese Frosting

Orange Poppy Seed

Citrus and poppy seeds give this cake a crisp, fruity, and sweet taste—
perfect for your next brunch or special breakfast.

1 box yellow cake mix

2 Tbsp. poppy seeds

1 medium orange, juiced

2 Tbsp. orange zest

½ tsp. orange extract

2 eggs

½ cup milk

Mix all ingredients together in a large bowl.

Pour batter into paper liners and fill ¾ full.

Bake at 350 degrees for 15–18 minutes. Remove and allow to cool completely on a wire rack.

Frosting Suggestions

Cream Cheese Frosting with ½ teaspoon orange extract

Peach Cobbler

There is a favorite peach cobbler recipe in my family. Here is a very easy version in a single serving cupcake form.

1 box yellow cake mix

3 eggs

½ cup butter, melted

½ cup milk

1 tsp. vanilla extract

1 tsp. cinnamon

1 tsp. nutmeg

1 pound sliced peaches (canned or fresh), peeled and drained

2 Tbsp. sugar

Mix together cake mix, eggs, butter, milk, vanilla, cinnamon, and nutmeg.

Place sliced peaches in a large bowl and sprinkle sugar on top. Toss gently and set aside.

Pour about 2 tablespoons batter in the bottom of each paper liner. Place equal amount of peaches on top of each batter-filled paper liner. Fill the remaining paper liner ¾ full.

Bake at 350 degrees for 18–20 minutes or until cake springs back when lightly touched.

Serve warm with ice cream or whipped cream.

Pear Upside Down

Pears are in season at fall time. This cupcake takes advantage of fruit when it is harvested. Canned pears work well too.

1 box white cake mix

2 eggs

½ cup oil

1 tsp. vanilla extract

¾ cup brown sugar

18–24 pear quarters, peeled

Mix together cake mix, eggs, oil, and vanilla. Set aside. Crumble brown sugar in the bottom of the paper liners.

Top the sugar with 1–2 pear quarters. Pour batter on the top of the pears, and fill ¾ full.

Bake at 350 degrees for 15–18 minutes. Immediately turn cupcakes upside down on a serving platter. Carefully remove paper liners—they will be hot!

Serve with a scoop of ice cream.

Piña Colada

with Whipped Cream

Piña Colada

Light and refreshing, these cupcakes will truly satisfy your sweet tooth. They're almost as good as the real thing.

- 1 box yellow cake mix
- 3 eggs
- 1 tsp. coconut extract
- ½ cup buttermilk
- 1 small can crushed pineapple
- 1 recipe whipped cream

Mix together cake mix, eggs, coconut extract, buttermilk, and pineapple with juice.

Pour batter into paper liners and fill ¾ full.

Bake at 350 degrees for 15–18 minutes or until cake springs back when lightly touched. Remove from pan and allow to cool on a wire rack.

Frosting Suggestions

Whipped Cream

Pineapple Upside Down

Pineapple Upside Down

This cupcake is best when served warm (upside down) with a scoop of ice cream. An easy dessert for a summer luau or any special occasion.

1 box yellow cake mix

3 eggs

1 can pineapple chunks, drained and juice saved for cake

pineapple juice from pineapple chunks, plus milk to equal 1 cup

¾ cup brown sugar

1 recipe whipped cream

maraschino cherries for garnish

Mix together cake mix, eggs, and pineapple juice plus milk to equal 1 cup. Beat until smooth.

Divide brown sugar between all paper liners equally. Place pineapple chunks in paper liner. Top with cake batter and fill ¾ full.

Bake at 350 degrees for 15–18 minutes or until cake springs back when lightly touched. Immediately flip each cupcake over onto a large platter and remove paper liner carefully—they will be hot!

Serve with whipped cream and garnish with a cherry.

Frosting Suggestions

Whipped Cream

Pink Lemonade

*This is a perfect treat for summertime. What if you made a
batch for your kids to sell at their next lemonade stand?
They wouldn't last very long!*

1 box white cake mix

⅓ cup pink lemonade
concentrate

½ cup buttermilk

3 eggs

2–3 drops red food
coloring

Mix together all ingredients until smooth.

Pour batter into paper liners and fill ¾
full.

Bake 15–18 minutes at 350 degrees
or until cake springs back when lightly
touched.

Cool completely before frosting.

Frosting Suggestions

Cream Cheese • Pink Lemonade Cream • Whipped Cream

Sour Cream Blueberry

with Whipped Cream

Sour Cream Blueberry

This cupcake has an eye-catching presentation. It is truly picture-perfect.

- 1 box yellow cake mix
- 2 eggs
- 1 cup sour cream
- 1 tsp. vanilla extract
- powdered sugar to garnish
- 1 recipe whipped cream
- 1 cup fresh or frozen blueberries

Mix together cake mix, eggs, sour cream, and vanilla.

Pour into paper liners and fill ¾ full.

Bake at 350 degrees for 15–18 minutes. Cupcake tops will not be rounded.

Remove from pan and allow to cool completely on a wire rack.

Dust top with powdered sugar and serve with a dollop of whipped cream and blueberries to garnish.

Frosting Suggestions

Whipped Cream

Strawberry Cheesecake

Cheesecake, yummy cheesecake! Whenever I can choose my dessert,
I pick cheesecake every time!

- 1 box white cake mix
- 3 eggs
- 1 cup milk
- 1 tsp. vanilla extract
- 1 package (8-oz.) cream cheese, softened
- 1 cup sugar
- 2 cups whipped topping
- 1 cup sliced strawberries for garnish

Mix together cake mix, eggs, milk, and vanilla. Pour batter in paper liners and fill ¾ full.

Bake at 350 degrees for 15–18 minutes or until cake springs back when touched lightly. Remove from pan and allow to cool completely. Cut top portion off and set aside to make a small cavity in each cupcake.

In a large mixing bowl, cream together sugar, cream cheese, and whipped topping. Spoon filling into each hole in the cupcake, gently replacing the top of the cake to seal.

Frost and garnish with strawberries.

Frosting Suggestions

Whipped Cream • Vanilla Buttercream

Strawberry Shortcake
with Whipped Cream

Strawberry Shortcake

This dessert is known for its light and fresh taste. A summer staple for an after-dinner treat, especially when strawberries are in season.

- 1 package white cake mix
- 2 eggs
- 1 cup whipping cream
- 1 tsp. vanilla extract
- ¼ tsp. salt
- 2 cups diced strawberries
- 2 Tbsp. sugar
- 1 recipe whipped cream

Add sugar to strawberries in a medium bowl. Stir and set aside. Mix together cake mix, eggs, whipping cream, vanilla, and salt and beat until light and fluffy.

Pour 1–2 tablespoons batter into paper liners. Add 2 tablespoons strawberry mixture on top. Cover strawberries with more batter and fill ¾ full. Save extra strawberries for garnish.

Bake at 350 degrees for 15–18 minutes or until cake springs back when lightly touched. Allow cake to cool slightly before serving with whipped cream and strawberries.

Frosting Suggestions

Whipped Cream

Tutti Frutti

This cupcake is a take on the ever-so-popular holiday treat. But my version is the best yet!

1 box yellow cake mix
3 eggs
¼ cup oil
1 tsp. vanilla extract
1 can fruit cocktail with juice

Mix together cake mix, eggs, oil, vanilla, and fruit cocktail. Pour into paper liners and fill ¾ full.

Bake at 350 degrees for 15–18 minutes until cake springs back when lightly touched. Remove from oven and cool on a wire rack.

Serve with a scoop of ice cream or whipped cream.

Vanilla Pudding Poppy Seed

This is a great cupcake for a brunch or a late afternoon snack. You can enjoy the softness of the sweet cupcake with or without frosting.

1 box yellow cake mix

1 package (4-oz.) vanilla pudding mix (powder only)

2 Tbsp. poppy seeds

3 eggs

1 cup milk

1 tsp. vanilla extract

Mix together cake mix, pudding mix, poppy seeds, eggs, milk, and vanilla. Pour into paper liners and fill ¾ full.

Bake at 350 degrees for 15–18 minutes or until cake springs back when lightly touched. Remove from the oven and cool on a wire rack.

Frosting Suggestions

Vanilla Buttercream

White Chocolate Strawberry

The name of this cupcake says it all, doesn't it?

- 2 cups white chocolate chips
- 1 box white cake mix
- 2 eggs
- 1 cup milk
- 1 tsp. vanilla extract
- white chocolate chunks for garnish
- strawberries for garnish

Melt white chocolate in the microwave 20 seconds at a time, until smooth. Stir in between. Do not overheat chocolate (it burns easily). Set aside to cool.

Mix together cake mix, eggs, milk, and vanilla. Fold melted white chocolate into batter and stir to combine. Fill paper liners ¾ full.

Bake at 350 degrees for 15–18 minutes. Remove from oven and cool completely on a wire rack.

Frost and top with white chocolate chunks and strawberries to garnish.

Frosting Suggestions

White Chocolate Mousse • Whipped Cream • Vanilla Buttercream

Yogurt Parfait

The yogurt in this cupcake creates a unique tang and flavor. I never thought I'd offer my children a cupcake for breakfast, but this one is really good!

- 1 box white cake mix
- 1 (6-oz.) container of vanilla yogurt
- ½ cup milk
- 2 eggs
- 1½ cups granola
- 2 cups diced berries (blackberries, strawberries, etc.) for garnish

Mix together cake mix, yogurt, milk, and eggs. Fold in ¾ cup granola. Pour into paper liners and fill ¾ full. Sprinkle unbaked cupcakes with remaining granola.

Bake at 350 degrees for 15–18 minutes until cake springs back when lightly touched. Remove from oven and cool.

Top with diced berries just before serving.

The Sweetness of Chocolate

Black Forest
Burnt Almond Fudge
Chocolate Almond
Chocolate Angels
Chocolate Caramel Surprise
Chocolate Chip Mint
Chocolate Chip Oatmeal
Chocolate Chip Zucchini
Chocolate Cinnamon
Chocolate Cookie Dough
Chocolate Cream
Chocolate Fudge Brownie
Chocolate Mayonnaise
Chocolate Peanut Butter Crumble

Chocolate Peanut Butter Cup
Chocolate Raspberry Trifle
Cookies and Cream Dream
Double Fudge
Give Me S'more
It's a Rocky Road
Little Earthquake
Melting Surprise
Mint Patty Brownie
Nanaimo Brownie
Oreo Cookie
Slippery Butterfingers
Sour Cream Chocolate
White Chocolate Vanilla

Black Forest
with Chocolate Ganache

Black Forest

As a child, I watched my grandpa eat chocolate-covered cherries as a special treat. Many years later we discovered he only ate them because we gave them to him as a present. He truly didn't like them at all! But I sure enjoyed them.

- 1 box chocolate cake mix
- 3 eggs
- ½ cup sour cream
- 1 tsp. almond extract
- 1 large can cherry pie filling (set aside)
- 1 cup filling for topping

Mix together cake mix, eggs, sour cream, almond extract, and pie filling until cake mix is moist. Do not overmix. Pour batter evenly in paper liners and fill ¾ full.

Bake at 350 degrees for 17–19 minutes or until barely done in center. Remove from oven and allow to cool completely on a rack.

Frost cupcakes, making a slight edge around the cupcake to hold the cherry filling.

Add 1 tablespoon filling to the top of each cupcake.

Frosting Suggestions

Chocolate Buttercream · Chocolate Ganache

Burnt Almond Fudge

Is your mouth watering after reading this cupcake title? Can you taste the roasted almonds and rich, creamy fudge? Why not make this cupcake for dessert tonight?

1 box dark chocolate
  cake mix

2 eggs

1 cup half and half

1 tsp. almond extract

2 cups chocolate
  chunks or
  chocolate chips

1 cup slivered
  almonds, roasted

Combine cake mix, eggs, half and half, and extract. Fold chocolate chunks and roasted almonds into batter. Pour into paper liners and fill ¾ full.

Bake at 350 degrees for 15–18 minutes or until cake springs back when lightly touched. Remove from oven and cool on a wire rack.

Frosting Suggestions

Chocolate Ganache • Chocolate Buttercream

Chocolate Almond

Almond is a perfect pairing with chocolate.

1 box chocolate cake mix

1 tsp. almond extract

1 cup chocolate chips

3 eggs

1 cup milk

1 cup slivered almonds
   for garnish

Combine all ingredients except slivered almonds. Fill paper liners ¾ full.

Bake at 350 degrees for 15–18 minutes or until top of cupcake springs back when lightly touched. Remove from oven and cool completely on a rack.

Frost cooled cupcakes and top with slivered almonds.

Frosting Suggestions

Chocolate Buttercream · Chocolate Mousse

Chocolate Angels

These chocolate cupcakes are light and airy—
a delicious dessert or treat anytime.

- 1 angel food cake mix
- ⅓ cup cocoa
- 1¼ cups water
- 1 recipe whipped cream
- strawberries (fresh or frozen) for garnish

Put cake mix and cocoa in a glass or metal bowl and whisk until combined. Add water and beat on low speed until moistened. Mix on medium speed for 1 minute.

Pour batter into paper liners and fill ⅔ full.

Bake at 350 degrees for 20–30 minutes or until lightly golden brown. Immediately remove from pan and cool on a wire rack. Serve with a dollop of whipped cream and strawberries.

Frosting Suggestions

Whipped Cream • Chocolate Mousse • White Chocolate Mousse

Chocolate Caramel Surprise

Chocolate Caramel Surprise

For all you caramel lovers, this is your cupcake of choice! Serve these little cakes with frosting, or a little warm with a dusting of powdered sugar and whipped cream on the side.

1 box chocolate cake mix

2 eggs

½ cup milk

½ cup oil

1 tsp. vanilla extract

1 package chocolate covered caramels

Mix together cake mix, eggs, milk, oil, and vanilla until light and fluffy.

Line cupcake pan with paper liners. Layer a spoonful of cake batter. Add 1–2 chocolate caramels on top of the batter. Fill paper liners with cake mix until ¾ full.

Bake at 350 degrees for 15–18 minutes or until cake springs back when lightly touched.

Frosting Suggestions

Caramel Cream • Chocolate Buttercream • Chocolate Ganache

Chocolate Chip Mint

One of my favorite ice cream flavors is chocolate chip mint. Why not make a cupcake with the same great taste? Mint and chocolate are the perfect combination.

3 eggs

1 cup milk

1 box chocolate cake mix

1 tsp. mint extract

1¼ cups mini chocolate chips (semi-sweet is best)

In a medium mixing bowl, whisk eggs until fluffy. Add milk and stir. Pour dry cake mix into egg mixture and stir until combined. Do not overstir. Add mint flavoring and 1 cup of the mini chocolate chips.

Pour batter into paper liners and fill ¾ full.

Bake at 350 degrees for 15–18 minutes or until cake springs back when lightly touched with your finger. Remove from pan and place cupcakes on a rack to cool.

Frost with desired frosting and sprinkle remaining chocolate chips on top.

Frosting Suggestions

White Chocolate Mint • Chocolate Buttercream

Chocolate Chip Oatmeal

Chocolate chips in oatmeal cake with numerous possibilities for frosting. You can take this cupcake and make it all your own.

- 1 box chocolate cake mix
- 2 eggs
- 1 cup quick oats
- ½ cup milk
- ¼ cup oil
- 1 tsp. vanilla extract
- 1 cup chocolate chips

Mix together all ingredients until batter is moistened. Pour into paper liners and fill ¾ full.

Bake at 350 degrees for 15–18 minutes or until cake springs back when lightly touched. Remove from the oven and cool completely.

Frosting Suggestions

Chocolate Ganache · Chocolate Buttercream
Chocolate Sour Cream · Vanilla Buttercream

Chocolate Chip Zucchini

I'm always looking for ways to use zucchini from my garden. My kids beg me to make this recipe. I don't mind making this sweet treat because it is full of vegetables! It also freezes well, without the frosting.

1 box chocolate cake mix

3 eggs

½ cup oil

1 cup grated zucchini

1 tsp. vanilla extract

1 cup chocolate chips

Mix together all ingredients until well combined. Pour into paper cupcake liners and fill ¾ full.

Bake at 350 degrees for 15–18 minutes or until cake springs back when lightly touched. Cool completely on a wire rack.

Frosting Suggestions

Chocolate Buttercream · Chocolate Ganache

Chocolate Cinnamon

Surprisingly, chocolate and cinnamon taste great together.
And cinnamon has been proven to be good for you.
So eat one, and don't feel too guilty!

- 1 box dark chocolate cake mix
- 2 eggs
- 1 cup milk
- 1 tsp. vanilla extract
- 2 Tbsp. cinnamon

Mix together all ingredients. Pour into paper liners to ¾ full.

Bake at 350 degrees for 15–18 minutes or until cake springs back when lightly touched. Remove from oven and cool completely.

Frosting Suggestions

Chocolate Ganache • Chocolate Buttercream

Chocolate Cookie Dough

The sweetness of cookie dough and a light, fluffy cupcake together is awesome. Mini cupcakes are a great after-school treat and a hit on a tray at a party.

- 1 box chocolate cake mix
- 3 eggs
- 1 Tbsp. milk
- 1 tsp. vanilla extract
- 1 package ready-made chocolate chip cookie dough
- 1 recipe whipped cream
- 1 cup mini chocolate chips for garnish

Combine cake mix, eggs, vanilla, and milk. Drop 1 tablespoon of batter into the paper liners, filling all 24. Pour the remaining batter on top of cookie dough filling and fill ¾ full.

Bake at 350 degrees for 15–18 minutes or until cake springs back when lightly touched. Remove and cool on a wire rack.

Top cooled cupcakes with whipped cream and mini chocolate chips.

Frosting Suggestions
Whipped Cream

Chocolate Cream
with Chocolate Ganache Frosting

Chocolate Cream

Chocolate cream cupcakes are simple to prepare,
yet elegant and full of rich chocolate flavors.

- 1 box chocolate cake mix
- 3 eggs
- 1 cup sour cream
- 2 cups heavy whipping cream
- ¼ cup powdered sugar
- ½ cup grated chocolate for garnish

Mix together cake mix, eggs, and sour cream until smooth.

Bake at 350 degrees for 15–18 minutes or until cake springs back when lightly touched.

Cool completely on a wire rack. When cooled, cut the top off and pull out some of the cake filling, leaving a solid wall of cake to support the filling. Whip the cream until stiff peaks form and add powdered sugar. Add whipped cream by the spoonful to the holes of all cupcakes and top with cupcake lid. Frost with desired frosting and garnish with grated chocolate.

Frosting Suggestions

Whipped Cream · Chocolate Buttercream · Chocolate Ganache

Chocolate Fudge Brownie

A good brownie can make a hungry person happy. Here's a dark chocolate brownie that takes the cake!

- 1 dark chocolate brownie mix (family size)
- ¼ cup water
- ⅓ cup oil
- 2 eggs
- 1 tsp. almond extract
- 2 cups semi–sweet chocolate chunks

Mix together all ingredients. Pour batter into paper liners and fill ¾ full.

Bake at 350 degrees for 13–15 minutes until soft, but not too wiggly. The middle will be gooey and delicious.

Serve warm with ice cream or frost after completely cooling on a wire rack.

Frosting Suggestions

Chocolate Ganache · Chocolate Buttercream
Peanut Butter · Cream Cheese

Chocolate Mayonnaise

My mom makes this cake for special family parties, and we usually have it for a birthday celebration. What makes this cake even more special is the cream cheese frosting. Trust me on this one!

- 1 box chocolate cake mix
- 1 cup mayonnaise (you can use reduced fat)
- ¼ cup water
- 1 tsp. vanilla extract
- 1 recipe cream cheese frosting

Mix together cake mix, mayonnaise, water, and vanilla. Pour batter into paper liners and fill ¾ full.

Bake at 350 degrees for 15–18 minutes or until cake springs back when lightly touched. Remove and cool on a wire rack.

Frost with cream cheese frosting.

Frosting Suggestions

Cream Cheese

Chocolate Peanut Butter Crumble

Chocolate Peanut Butter Crumble

I love the taste of chocolate and peanut butter together—chocolate and peanut butter cookies, peanut butter with chocolate syrup on ice cream, a spoonful of peanut butter with some chocolate chips sprinkled on top! Is your mouth watering like mine is now? This is my favorite cupcake. I hope it will become one of yours too!

1 box chocolate cake mix, ½ cup reserved

3 eggs

1 cup milk

2 cups peanut butter chips

½ cup quick oats

4 Tbsp. butter, softened

ice cream

chocolate syrup

Mix together cake mix, eggs, and milk. In a separate bowl, place peanut butter chips, oats, butter, and remaining ½ cup reserved cake mix. Mix together with a fork until small crumbles appear. Pour batter in paper liners and fill ⅔ full. Top with a spoonful of peanut butter crumbles, dividing evenly among all cupcakes.

Bake at 350 degrees for 18–20 minutes. Cake will be uneven on top. Serve with a garnish of ice cream on the top of these warm cupcakes, drizzled with chocolate syrup.

Chocolate Peanut Butter Cup

with Chocolate Buttercream Frosting

Chocolate Peanut Butter Cup

My neighbor said these cupcakes are sinful.
But believe me, they are worth every bite.

1 box chocolate
    cake mix

3 eggs

1 cup milk

1 bag chocolate
    peanut butter
    cups

Mix together cake mix, eggs, and milk. Pour 2 tablespoons batter into paper liners and place a peanut butter cup on top. Fill paper liners ¾ full.

Bake at 350 degrees for 15–18 minutes or until the cake springs back when lightly touched. Remove from oven and allow to cool on a wire rack. When completely cooled, frost.

Frosting Suggestions

Peanut Butter · Chocolate Buttercream

Chocolate Raspberry Trifle

with Whipped Cream

Chocolate Raspberry Trifle

Some of my friends ask me to make a chocolate raspberry trifle when we go to their home for dinner and dessert. Here is a smaller version, cupcake style.

1 chocolate cake mix

1 (4-oz.) package pudding powder

2 eggs

½ cup milk

1 recipe chocolate ganache

1 cup raspberries for garnish

Mix together cake mix, pudding powder, eggs, and milk. Pour into paper liners and fill ¾ full.

Bake at 350 degrees for 15–18 minutes or until cake springs back when lightly touched. Remove from the oven and cool on a wire rack.

Frost with chocolate ganache frosting and top with raspberries.

Frosting Suggestions

Chocolate Ganache · Chocolate Buttercream · Whipped Cream
Peanut Butter · Cream Cheese

Cookies and Cream Dream

with Vanilla Buttercream Frosting

Cookies and Cream Dream

Cookies and cream make anything taste great! These cupcakes go so fast after they're baked—be sure to hide a few for yourself.

- 1 box chocolate cake mix
- 1 cup sour cream
- 3 eggs
- 1 tsp. vanilla extract
- 18–24 whole chocolate sandwich cookies
- 12 chocolate sandwich cookies, crumbled
- 1 recipe vanilla buttercream frosting

Mix together cake mix, sour cream, eggs, and vanilla. Place a spoonful of batter on the bottom of each paper liner. Place a whole cookie on the bottom lying flat. Cover with remaining batter until ¾ full.

Bake at 350 degrees for 15–18 minutes. Allow cupcakes to cool on a rack completely.

Add crumbled cookies to buttercream frosting. Be generous and frost cupcakes nice and high.

Frosting Suggestions
Vanilla Buttercream

Double Fudge

Double Fudge

Is there really anything better than double fudge? The saying, "Hand over the chocolate and nobody gets hurt!" definitely applies to these little cakes.

- 1 box chocolate cake mix
- 3 eggs
- 1 cup heavy cream (or half and half)
- 1 cup semi–sweet chocolate chips, melted
- 1 cup semi–sweet chocolate chips

Mix together cake mix, eggs, and cream. Fold in melted chocolate chips and regular chocolate chips.

Pour batter into paper-lined cups and bake at 350 degrees for 15–18 minutes or until cupcakes spring back when lightly touched. Place on a rack and cool completely. Frost when cooled.

Frosting Suggestions

Chocolate Buttercream · Chocolate Ganache

Give Me S'more

Give Me S'more

S'mores are an essential part of camping. This cupcake brings part of the camping experience to your home anytime. If you want a bite-size treat, make these cupcakes with mini paper liners. Cut the graham crackers with a serrated knife for a custom fit.

- 1 box white cake mix
- 2 eggs
- 1 cup milk
- 1 bag large marshmallows
- 1 jar chocolate fudge sauce
- graham crackers (broken into squares)

Mix together cake mix, eggs, and milk. Pour into paper liners, filling ¾ full. Place one large marshmallow in the center of the unbaked cupcake and press down slightly to submerge marshmallow.

Bake at 350 degrees for 15–18 minutes or until marshmallow is golden and cake springs back when lightly touched. Remove from oven and cool on a wire rack.

Warm fudge sauce in the microwave and place a spoonful on top of each cupcake. Top with a graham cracker square.

It's a Rocky Road

Your cake and ice cream should go hand in hand, right? Why not mix this one up a bit too?

1 box chocolate cake
  mix
3 eggs
1 cup milk
1 cup chopped walnuts
1 cup chocolate chips
1–2 cups mini
  marshmallows

Mix together cake mix, eggs, and milk. Pour into paper liners and fill ¾ full.

Bake at 350 degrees for 12 minutes. Remove from oven. Quickly place walnuts, chocolate chips, and marshmallows on the center of each cupcake, dividing evenly.

Return to oven for 3–4 more minutes. Marshmallows will turn golden. Remove from oven and cool completely on a wire rack. Serve while still warm if desired.

Little Earthquake

This cupcake gets its name from the way it looks—a little shaky in the beginning, and a whole lot rocky (nutty) in the end.

1 box German chocolate cake mix

3 eggs

1 cup milk

1 cup shredded coconut

1 cup chopped pecans

4 Tbsp. butter, melted

½ package (4-oz.) cream cheese, softened

2 cups powdered sugar

Mix together cake mix, eggs, and milk. In a separate bowl, combine coconut and pecans. Divide and scatter nut mixture evenly in the bottom of each paper cupcake liner and set aside.

Cream together melted butter, cream cheese, and powdered sugar in a large bowl. Beat until light and smooth. Set aside.

Pour chocolate batter on top of nut mixture, filling each paper liner ⅔ full. Place a spoonful of cream cheese mix on top of the cupcake.

Bake at 350 degrees for 15–18 minutes. The topping will seem a little wobbly, but the cupcake will set as it cools. Remove cupcakes from oven and place on a rack until completely cool. Dust with powdered sugar before serving.

Melting Surprise
with Whipped Cream

Melting Surprise

This is a take on chocolate molten cake. But there is just something about unwrapping this little cupcake that is so much fun!

1 box chocolate cake mix

4 eggs

1 tsp. vanilla extract

½ cup sour cream

1 package (8-oz.) cream cheese, softened

½ cup sugar

1 cup semi–sweet chocolate chips, melted

Mix together cake mix, 3 eggs, vanilla, and sour cream. Set aside.

In a separate bowl, add softened cream cheese, 1 egg, sugar, and melted chocolate chips. Stir until combined well. Fill paper liners ¾ full. Add 1 teaspoon filling to the top of each cupcake.

Bake at 350 degrees for 20 minutes, being careful not to overbake.

Garnish with whipped cream and grated chocolate.

Frosting Suggestions

Whipped Cream

Mint Patty Brownie

These brownie cupcakes will be gone before they have cooled on your rack. Your family will smell them from a mile away!

- 1 dark chocolate brownie mix (family size)
- 2 eggs
- ¼ cup water
- 1 tsp. vanilla extract
- ⅓ cup oil
- 1 bag mint patties

Mix together brownie mix, eggs, water, vanilla, and oil. Stir until moistened. Pour about 2 tablespoons batter in every paper liner. Layer 2 mint patties in each liner. Top with remaining batter, filling ¾ full.

Bake at 350 degrees for 13–15 minutes until soft, but not too wiggly. The middle will be gooey and delicious.

Cool completely on wire rack. Dust with powdered sugar or frost.

Frosting Suggestions

Chocolate Buttercream • Chocolate Ganache
Chocolate Mousse • Whipped Cream

Nanaimo Brownie

Nanaimo Brownie

Several years ago on a trip with my husband, I came across a phenomenal treat in British Columbia called nanaimo bars. I have taken this brownie cupcake and added the traditional ingredients to make it shine. Holy cow!

- 1 box dark chocolate brownie mix (family size)
- 2 eggs
- ⅓ cup oil
- ½ cup water
- 1 cup shredded coconut
- 1 cup chopped almonds
- 2 cups heavy whipping cream
- ⅓ cup powdered sugar
- 4 Tbsp. Bird's custard powder
- 2 Tbsp. butter
- 4 Tbsp. semi–sweet chocolate chips

Combine brownie mix, eggs, oil, and water. Stir until moistened. In a separate bowl, combine coconut and chopped almonds.

Spoon nut mixture evenly throughout paper liners. Fill paper liners with brownie batter ¾ full.

Bake at 350 degrees for 13–15 minutes, until soft in the center. Remove and cool completely on a wire rack.

Meanwhile, whip the cream until firm peaks form. Add custard powder and powdered sugar and combine well. Frost cooled cupcakes with the custard—be generous!

Melt butter and chocolate in a small bowl in the microwave. Be careful not to burn the chocolate. Stir every 20 seconds. Drizzle cooled chocolate over the custard cream topping.

Oreo Cookie

My children have a favorite treat at Grandma's house—Oreos and milk. Here's a cupcake with my children in mind. Those chocolate smiles warm my heart every time!

- 1 box chocolate cake mix
- 3 eggs
- 1 cup milk
- 24 Oreo cookies

Mix cake mix, eggs, and milk. Pour batter into paper liners and fill ½ full. Place a whole Oreo cookie on top and push down slightly to submerge. Cover with remaining batter and fill ¾ full.

Bake at 350 degrees for 15–18 minutes or until cake springs back when lightly touched. Remove from the oven and cool completely.

Frosting Suggestions

Chocolate Ganache • Chocolate Buttercream

Slippery Butterfingers

*My husband came up with this idea—crushed candy bars baked
into the actual cupcake to add texture dimension to every bite.
It's delicious!*

1 box yellow cake mix

3 eggs

¼ cup oil

½ cup milk

1 tsp. vanilla extract

2 cups crushed
   Butterfinger candy bar

Mix together cake mix, eggs, oil, milk, and vanilla. Add 1 cup crushed candy to batter. Pour into paper liners and fill ¾ full.

Bake at 350 degrees for 15–18 minutes or until cake springs back when lightly touched. Remove from oven and cool completely.

Frost and top with remaining crushed candy bars.

Frosting Suggestions

Chocolate Buttercream • Vanilla Buttercream

Sour Cream Chocolate

Sour cream is so good in both the cake and frosting. Make this cupcake and pair it with chocolate sour cream frosting, or whichever frosting pleases your taste.

1 box dark chocolate
  cake mix

2 eggs

½ cup vegetable oil

1 cup sour cream

1 tsp. vanilla extract

Mix together all ingredients. Pour into paper liners and fill ¾ full.

Bake at 350 degrees for 15–18 minutes or until cake springs back when lightly touched. Remove from oven and cool completely.

Frosting Suggestions

Chocolate Sour Cream · Chocolate Buttercream

White Chocolate Vanilla

Even though white chocolate technically isn't chocolate, it pairs so well with vanilla. When you place a generous layer of frosting and chunks of white chocolate on top as a garnish, it's like a dream come true.

1 box white cake mix

1 cup white chocolate chips

1 tsp. vanilla extract

1 cup milk

2 eggs

½ cup oil

1 cup white chocolate chunks

Mix together cake mix, white chocolate chips, vanilla, milk, eggs, and oil. Fill paper liners ¾ full.

Bake at 350 degrees for 15–18 minutes or until cake springs back when lightly touched. Allow to cool completely on wire rack.

Frost with white chocolate frosting and garnish with white chocolate chunks.

Frosting Suggestions
White Chocolate

Holiday Treats

Angel Food Toasted Coconut
Bridal Party
Candy Cane
Churro
Cinnamon Spice Buttermilk
Donut Cupcake
Ginger Carrot Cake

Gingerbread Cookie
Harvest Pumpkin
Ice Cream Sandwich
Independence Vanilla Cream
Pecan Pie
Red Velvet Valentine
Root Beer Float

Angel Food Toasted Coconut
with Vanilla Buttercream Frosting

Angel Food Toasted Coconut

This cupcake is so beautiful, you almost don't want to eat it. The toasted coconut on top is eye-catching and gives a crunchy and chewy texture to the cake.

1 box angel food
cake mix

1¼ cups water

1½ cups toasted
coconut flakes

1 recipe vanilla
buttercream
frosting

Mix together cake mix and water on low until moistened. Slowly increase speed until batter is fluffy and light. Pour batter into paper liners.

Bake at 350 degrees for 20–25 minutes or until cake is light and golden in color. Remove from oven and cool on a wire rack.

Meanwhile, place coconut flakes on a cookie sheet, spreading out in a single layer. Bake at 400 degrees, checking every minute. It will only take about 2–4 minutes. The coconut will become fragrant and brown very easily. Set aside to cool.

Frost cakes with vanilla buttercream frosting and top with toasted coconut.

Frosting Suggestions

Vanilla Buttercream

Bridal Party

with Vanilla Buttercream Frosting

Bridal Party

This cupcake is so pretty and delicate. Little edible pansies liven up this cake and make it special and unforgettable. You can paint a small amount of water (with a small paint brush) on the petals of the flower and dust with sugar crystals to give it an extra special touch.

- 1 box white cake mix
- 3 eggs
- 1 cup milk or sour cream
- 1 tsp. vanilla extract, lemon, or almond extract
- edible flowers

Mix together all ingredients, except edible flowers. Pour batter into paper liners and fill ¾ full.

Bake at 350 degrees for 15–18 minutes or until cakes are light golden brown and spring back when lightly touched. Remove from oven and cool completely on a wire rack.

Frost when cooled. Garnish with edible flowers.

Frosting Suggestions

White Chocolate Mousse • Vanilla Buttercream
Whipped Cream • Cream Cheese

Candy Cane

Make these for any Christmas gathering, and please your friends and family. The white chocolate chunks and crushed peppermint candy add to the taste and texture of the little cake.

1 box white cake mix

3 eggs

1 cup milk

1 tsp. vanilla extract

1 recipe vanilla buttercream frosting

peppermint candy for garnish

1 cup white chocolate chunks for garnish

Mix together cake mix, eggs, milk, and vanilla. Pour batter into the paper liners and fill ¾ full.

Bake at 350 degrees for 15–18 minutes or until cakes are light golden brown. Remove from oven and cool completely on a wire rack.

Frost with vanilla buttercream frosting and top generously with white chocolate chunks and crushed peppermint candies.

Frosting Suggestions

Vanilla Buttercream

Churro

Every time I eat a churro, I think of Disneyland. Churros are warm and chewy, and covered with cinnamon and sugar. These cupcakes are best served warm.

- 1 box white cake mix
- 3 eggs
- 1 cup sour cream
- 1 tsp. vanilla extract
- ¾ cup sugar
- 2 Tbsp. cinnamon
- 4 Tbsp. butter, melted

Mix together cake mix, eggs, sour cream, and vanilla. Put 2 tablespoons of batter in each paper liner.

In a separate bowl, combine white sugar and cinnamon. Stir until combined well. Sprinkle 1 teaspoon sugar mix on top of cake batter. Top with remaining batter and fill ¾ full.

Bake at 350 degrees for 15–18 minutes or until cake springs back when lightly touched. Remove from oven and set aside.

With a pastry brush or spoon, place melted butter on top of cupcakes. Sprinkle remaining sugar mix, dividing evenly among all cupcakes. Serve warm.

Cinnamon Spice Buttermilk

This cupcake is sweet and spicy, with a little tang from the buttermilk. The perfect tastes of fall, or a special treat anytime.

- 1 box spice cake mix
- 3 eggs
- 1 cup buttermilk
- 2 tsp. vanilla extract
- 1 tsp. cinnamon

Mix together all ingredients. Pour batter into the paper liners, filling ¾ full.

Bake at 350 degrees for 15–18 minutes or until cakes are light golden brown. Remove from oven and cool completely on a wire rack.

Frost with desired frosting.

Frosting Suggestions

Cream Cheese • Orange Cream Cheese • Vanilla Buttercream

Donut Cupcake

Sweet donuts are the ultimate treat. Can you ever just eat one?
These cupcakes have endless possibilities for frosting. Berries or
whipped cream sweeten these little cakes even more.

- 1 box yellow cake mix
- 1 (4-oz.) package vanilla instant pudding mix (powder only)
- ¼ cup mashed potatoes (can use instant)
- 1 tsp. vanilla extract
- 2 eggs
- 1 cup milk

Mix together all ingredients until well combined. Fill paper liners ¾ full.

Bake at 350 degrees for 18–20 minutes or until cake springs back when lightly touched. Remove from oven and allow to cool on a wire rack.

Cool completely before frosting.

Frosting Suggestions

Caramel Cream • Vanilla Buttercream • Chocolate Buttercream

Ginger Carrot Cake

with Orange Cream Cheese Frosting

Ginger Carrot Cake

*My sister said if I were to make a cupcake cookbook, I must include
a really good carrot cake recipe. Sis, this one's for you!*

1 box carrot cake mix

3 eggs

1 cup milk

1 tsp. cinnamon

1 tsp. vanilla extract

1 tsp. ginger

1 cup raisins (optional)

1 cup chopped
walnuts (optional)

Mix together cake mix, eggs, milk, cinnamon, vanilla, ginger, raisins (optional), and nuts (optional). Pour batter into paper liners and fill ¾ full.

Bake at 350 degrees for 15–18 minutes or until cake springs back when lightly touched. Remove from oven and cool completely.

Frost with desired frosting. To garnish, sprinkle lightly with ground cinnamon.

Frosting Suggestions
Cream Cheese • Orange Cream Cheese • Vanilla Buttercream

Gingerbread Cookie
with Cream Cheese Frosting

Gingerbread Cookie

Nothing says it's autumn better than a good gingerbread cookie.
Now, nothing says it better than a gingerbread cookie cupcake!

- 1 box spice cake mix
- 3 eggs
- ⅓ cup molasses
- ⅓ cup oil
- ½ cup milk

Mix together cake mix, eggs, molasses, oil, and milk. Pour into paper liners and fill ¾ full.

Bake at 350 degrees for 15–18 minutes or until the cake springs back when lightly touched.

Frosting Suggestions
Cream Cheese • Orange Cream Cheese

Harvest Pumpkin
with Cream Cheese Frosting

Harvest Pumpkin

My father tasted the combination of chocolate and butterscotch chips in a pumpkin cookie. This treat will surprise your taste buds and get you ready for fall.

1 box spice cake mix

1 cup pumpkin puree

1 tsp. vanilla extract

2 eggs

½ cup milk

1 cup chocolate chips

1 cup butterscotch chips

Mix together all ingredients. Pour batter into paper liners and fill ¾ full.

Bake at 350 degrees for 15–18 minutes or until cakes are light golden brown. Remove from the oven and cool completely on a wire rack.

Frosting Suggestions

Chocolate Ganache · Chocolate Buttercream
Cream Cheese · Vanilla Buttercream

Ice Cream Sandwich

Ice Cream Sandwich

Cake and ice cream go hand in hand. Mixing these two together is a no-nonsense approach to dessert. You can have your cake and eat your ice cream too!

- 1 box white or chocolate cake mix
- 3 eggs
- 1 cup milk
- 1 tsp. vanilla extract
- 2 cups ice cream, your favorite flavor

Mix together cake mix, eggs, milk, and vanilla.

Bake at 350 degrees for 15–18 minutes or until cake springs back when lightly touched. Remove from oven and allow to cool completely on a wire rack.

When cooled, remove the wrapper and cut the cupcake in half horizontally. Scoop your ice cream onto the bottom layer of cupcake. Top with other half.

Freeze 30 minutes to 1 hour to harden the ice cream. Frost just before serving.

Frosting Suggestions

Chocolate Buttercream · Vanilla Buttercream · Peanut Butter

Independence Vanilla Cream

with Whipped Cream

Independence Vanilla Cream

These little cakes make a great dessert for a Fourth of July barbecue or any gathering during the summertime.

1 box white cake mix

3 eggs

1 cup milk

1 tsp. vanilla extract

1 recipe whipped cream

strawberries, blueberries, or raspberries for garnish (fresh or frozen)

Mix together cake mix, eggs, milk, and vanilla. Pour the batter into paper liners, filling ¾ full.

Bake at 350 degrees for 15–18 minutes or until cakes are light golden brown. Remove from oven and cool completely on a wire rack.

Frost generously and spoon fresh or frozen berries over the top just before serving.

Frosting Suggestions

Whipped Cream · White Chocolate Mousse

Pecan Pie

Can you taste this one already? Your mouth is watering, and you're thinking of the last time you ate this wonderful pie. Your next memory should be eating this delightful version, cupcake style. Come on, it's really simple!

1 box butter pecan cake mix

1 cup whole milk

1 cube butter, softened

5 eggs

1 tsp. vanilla extract

¾ cup dark corn syrup

¼ cup packed brown sugar

1½ cups roasted pecans, chopped or halved

Mix together cake mix, milk, butter, 3 eggs, and vanilla. Pour about 2 tablespoons into paper liners.

In a separate bowl, mix together corn syrup, brown sugar, chopped pecans, and 2 eggs. Divide nut mixture evenly among all the cupcakes, about 1 spoonful each. Fill the paper liners ¾ full.

Bake at 350 degrees for 18–20 minutes or until cake springs back when lightly touched. Allow cakes to cool completely before serving. This allows the filling to set. If you don't want to frost, dust with powdered sugar and serve with a side of whipped cream.

Frosting Suggestions

Chocolate Buttercream • Vanilla Buttercream • Whipped Cream

Red Velvet Valentine

Make this special little cake for the ones you love. Pack it in their lunch or deliver it to work. What a great surprise! They will know you care and are thinking of them.

- 1 box dark chocolate cake mix or white cake mix
- 3 eggs
- 1 cup milk
- 1 small bottle of red food coloring
- 1 tsp. vanilla extract
- heart-shaped foil liners
- chocolate shaving or chunks for garnish

Mix together cake mix, eggs, milk, food coloring, and vanilla. Pour batter into heart-shaped special foil liners, filling ¾ full.

Bake at 350 degrees for 15–18 minutes or until cakes are light golden brown. Remove from oven and cool completely on a wire rack.

Frost and garnish with chocolate shavings or chunks.

Frosting Suggestions

Chocolate Ganache • Chocolate Mousse
Chocolate Buttercream • Whipped Cream

Root Beer Float

with Root Beer Buttercream Frosting

Root Beer Float

My father-in-law loved a good glass of root beer. When he started saying we didn't need to buy him anything for Christmas or his birthday, someone would always give him a duffle bag of root beer—a three-month supply. This cupcake is in honor of him!

1 white cake mix

1 cup of your favorite root beer

1 recipe vanilla buttercream

1 tsp. root beer flavoring

Mix together root beer and cake mix. Pour into paper liners and fill ¾ full.

Bake at 350 degrees for 15–18 minutes or until cake springs back when lightly touched. Remove from oven and allow to cool completely.

In a separate bowl, mix buttercream frosting and root beer flavoring. Frost cooled cupcakes.

Frosting Suggestions

Root Beer Buttercream

Theme Decorating

Banana Split

Bird's Nest

Birthday Candles

Birthday Presents

Butterfly

Candy Bar Party

Caterpillar

Christmas Tree

Creepy Spider

Dinosaurs on the Rocks

Easter Egg Basket

Easter Peeps

Flower Power

Fudge Sundae Cone

Holiday Wreath

Little Sheep

Lucky Green

New Year's Celebration

Picnic Cake in a Jar

Pumpkin

Rainbow

Spring Garden

Banana Split

Banana Split

This cupcake is so much fun to make, but even more fun to eat.

1 recipe of your favorite
    cupcake (18–24, baked
    and cooled)

1 recipe chocolate ganache

6 bananas, sliced

maraschino cherries

1 recipe whipped cream

chopped nuts (optional)

Top cupcakes with chocolate ganache and sliced bananas, dividing them evenly among all the cupcakes. Finish with cherries, whipped cream, and nuts (optional).

Bird's Nest

This is a fun way to display Easter eggs for a party. You can even place a toothpick with a nametag in each cupcake to personalize the cupcakes, or use them for place settings.

- 1 recipe of your favorite cupcake (18–24, baked and cooled)
- 1 recipe chocolate buttercream frosting
- 2 cups grated chocolate
- 1 bag chocolate egg candy

Generously frost cupcakes with chocolate buttercream frosting.

Top with a small handful of grated chocolate (enough to cover the frosting), making a small rim around the edge of the cupcake.

Place 3 chocolate eggs in the center of the "nest" of grated chocolate.

Birthday Candles
with Vanilla Buttercream Frosting

Birthday Candles

When my children talk about these cupcakes, their faces light up.
My son asked, "When can we blow them out?"

- 1 recipe of your favorite cupcake (18–24, baked and cooled)
- 1 recipe vanilla butter-cream frosting
- 1 bag Life Savers
- 1 box colored candles
- sprinkles

Frost cooled cupcakes with buttercream frosting. Center a Life Saver on top.

Place a candle through the center of the Life Saver.

Use sprinkles to garnish and add more color.

Frosting Suggestions
Vanilla Buttercream

Birthday Presents

Use this breathtaking display at the next birthday party you attend.
Presents are even better when you can eat them too!

- 1 recipe of your favorite cupcake (18–24, baked and cooled)
- 1 recipe vanilla buttercream frosting
- 18–24 square marshmallows (found in a specialty candy shop)
- sprinkles
- colored sugar
- small bowl of water
- paintbrush
- vine-style licorice for ribbon

Paint a small amount of water on each marshmallow square. Roll in colored sugar to coat. Set aside to dry.

Wrap each marshmallow present with licorice and tie in a loose knot or bow. Set marshmallows aside.

Frost cupcakes with buttercream frosting and top with sprinkles. Set finished marshmallow on top or off to the side, depending on your preference.

Butterfly

Butterflies are magical. This arrangement is fast and easy, and only takes a few minutes to prepare—and even fewer to decorate!

2 recipes of your favorite cupcake (36–48, baked and cooled)

2 recipes vanilla buttercream frosting

2 colors decorating sugars (i.e., dark pink, light pink, or lavender and pink)

green sprinkles or sugar

black vine licorice for antennae

large platter (upside down cookie sheet works really well) for cupcakes to be decorated and presented on

Frost cupcakes. Cover 5 cupcakes with green sugar or sprinkles to make your butterfly body. Place in a single layer on the middle of the platter. The top cupcake will be your head. Place the black licorice (2-in. length) through the side of the paper liner. You may need to cut a slit in the paper to fit the licorice in to make the antennae.

Divide remaining cupcakes evenly. Cover half with one color of sugar and the rest with the second color. Choose a color and make a larger outline or a large half circle for the top wing on one side and repeat on the other side. Use the second colored cupcakes for the smaller wings, repeating the same process. Fill in any holes with remaining cupcakes.

Candy Bar Party

This cupcake can be tailored to all those who attend a party. You can use it as a get-to-know-you game. Each guest chooses the candy bar that best describes him and places it on a cupcake without others seeing. The other guests then try to guess which cupcake belongs to which guest. The person who claims the cupcake has to tell why the candy bar best describes him.

1 recipe of your favorite cupcake (18–24, baked and cooled)

1 recipe vanilla buttercream frosting

1 package mini candy bars

Frost cooled cupcakes. You can either place the whole mini candy bar on the top, or stick it in the center, leaving some showing. You can also chop the candy bar into smaller pieces and sprinkle them on top.

Caterpillar

A simple but very creative way to arrange cupcakes. You can even use smashed chocolate sandwich cookies to make the dirt the caterpillar rests on.

1 recipe of your favorite cupcake (18–24, baked and cooled)

1 recipe vanilla buttercream frosting

green food coloring

green sprinkles

1 bag stick pretzels for legs

black gel icing to make the eyes (or black jelly beans)

large platter (upside down cookie sheet works really well) for cupcakes to be decorated and presented on

Combine icing and green food coloring and mix until icing is completely green. Frost cupcakes and cover with green sprinkles.

Arrange cupcakes in an "S" shape on your serving tray. Place 2 pretzels for the legs on each side of every cupcake. Place black jelly beans on the head for the eyes.

Christmas Tree

This is an easy way to get the kids involved with decorating and having a good time in the kitchen. It's never too early to start. Even my two-year-old can frost a cupcake—it's a masterpiece every time!

- 1 recipe of your favorite cupcake (18–24, baked and cooled)
- 1 recipe vanilla buttercream frosting
- large platter (upside down cookie sheet works really well) for cupcakes to be decorated and presented on
- green food coloring
- assorted candy to decorate the frosted tree

Mix together green food coloring and vanilla buttercream frosting.

Frost and place the cupcakes in rows, starting with the bottom row of 7 cupcakes, then 6, 5, and so on, ending with 1.

Place one last cupcake on the bottom center for the trunk.

Let the kids decorate the tree with all of the candy. This is a great job for them.

Creepy Spider

*This decorated cupcake is sure to give your little goblins
a fright on Halloween night!*

- 1 recipe of your favorite cupcake (18–24, baked and cooled)
- 1 recipe chocolate frosting
- 24 chocolate with chocolate cream-filled cookies
- black vine licorice

Frost cookies with chocolate ganache.

Cut 1½–2-in. pieces of licorice and stick in the sides of each of the cookies for the spider legs.

Place each leggy cookie on the center of frosted cupcake.

Dinosaurs
on the Rocks
with
Chocolate Buttercream Frosting

Dinosaurs on the Rocks

We all know a child who loves dinosaurs. These cupcakes are wonderful and easy to assemble. Plus, you can use the toy dinosaurs as party favors.

- 1 recipe of your favorite cupcake (18–24, baked and cooled)
- 1 recipe chocolate buttercream frosting
- 24 small plastic dinosaurs
- 1 bag rock candy

Frost cupcakes with chocolate frosting.

Top with rock candy and place a plastic dinosaur on each cupcake.

Frosting Suggestions
Chocolate Buttercream

Easter Egg Basket

Kids will love decorating these before Easter. This is a great hands-on project for any baker in training.

- 1 recipe of your favorite cupcake (18–24, baked and cooled)
- 1 recipe vanilla buttercream frosting
- green food coloring
- 1 cup shredded coconut
- 24 pipe cleaners in a variety of colors
- candy eggs for decorating

Add 3–4 drops green food coloring to vanilla buttercream frosting and mix until combined. Set aside.

In a separate bowl, add 2–3 drops green food coloring to coconut, stirring until all coconut has turned green. Frost cupcakes generously.

With your fingers, pat coconut onto wet frosting, making sure there are enough coats to make the coconut look like grass. Place your pipe cleaner on opposite sides of the cupcake, making a handle. Put candy in the center so it will look like a basket of goodies.

Easter Peeps

Nothing says Easter is close like a box of Peeps!

1 recipe of your favorite cupcake (18–24, baked and
cooled)

1 recipe vanilla buttercream
frosting

green food coloring

1 cup shredded coconut

3 medium packages of bunny
or chick Peeps

Add 3–4 drops green food coloring to vanilla buttercream frosting and mix until combined. Set aside.

Put coconut in a separate bowl and add 2–3 drops green food coloring, stirring until all coconut has turned green. Frost cupcakes generously.

With your fingers, pat coconut onto wet frosting, making sure there are enough coats to make the coconut look like grass. Place a Peep in the center of the cupcake and serve on a platter.

Flower Power

For springtime parties or to bring a bouquet of edible cupcake flowers to someone special, all you need are a few simple extra ingredients.

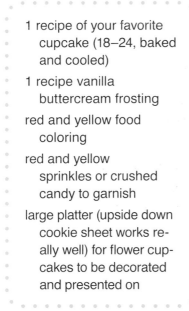

- 1 recipe of your favorite cupcake (18–24, baked and cooled)
- 1 recipe vanilla buttercream frosting
- red and yellow food coloring
- red and yellow sprinkles or crushed candy to garnish
- large platter (upside down cookie sheet works really well) for flower cupcakes to be decorated and presented on

Place buttercream frosting in a large bowl, minus about ¾ cup. Place ¾ cup frosting in a separate bowl. Add 1–3 drops yellow food coloring to ¾ cup frosting. Stir well until yellow food coloring has become even. Set aside.

For the larger amount of frosting, place 2–3 drops red food coloring and stir well until red coloring has become even. Set aside.

Using your offset spatula, frost yellow buttercream frosting onto 3 cupcakes. Place them spaced apart (for the petals of the flower to be placed around the center) on the platter.

Frost remaining cupcakes with red frosting. Place the red frosted cupcakes around the yellow ones.

Add sprinkles and embellish any way you'd like.

Fudge Sundae Cone

This is a fun twist on serving a cupcake. Try it sometime when you are in the mood for an ice cream cone. Just add the cupcakes!

1 recipe of your favorite chocolate cupcake (18–24, baked and cooled)

1 recipe chocolate ganache

vanilla ice cream

24 ice cream cones

Place a scoop of ice cream on each cupcake. Top with a cone, slightly tipped to the side.

Drizzle generously with chocolate ganache.

Holiday Wreath

Another fun decorating idea where the kids can help.

- 1 recipe of your favorite cupcake (18–24, baked and cooled)
- 1 recipe vanilla buttercream frosting
- large platter (upside down cookie sheet works really well) for cupcakes to be decorated and presented on
- green food coloring
- 1 bag red candy or chocolate-covered cherries (red shell)
- red vine licorice

Mix together green food coloring and buttercream frosting. Frost cupcakes and arrange in a circle, 2 rows deep.

Top with red candy or chocolate-covered cherries, placing several on each cupcake. Make a bow using licorice and place at the bottom, centered, or slightly off to the side.

Little Sheep

*Little Bo Peep won't lose all her sheep until it's time to
eat these cupcakes!*

- 1 recipe of your favorite
  cupcake (18–24, baked
  and cooled)
- 1 recipe vanilla buttercream
  frosting
- 1 bag large marshmallows
- 1 bag miniature
  marshmallows
- toothpicks
- black gel icing in a tube

Frost cupcakes with buttercream icing.

Place 1 large marshmallow on its side near
the edge of the cupcake. Secure with more
icing if needed.

Place mini marshmallows on cupcakes,
small sides down, and cover entire top of
cake. (This is the sheep's wool.)

Break one toothpick in half and secure
a mini marshmallow on one end of each
toothpick. Place these toothpicks (one
on each side) through the top of the large
marshmallow for the ears. With the black
gel icing, make two dots for the eyes.

Lucky Green

St. Patrick's Day is all about celebrating with friends and family.
Serve these cupcakes for dessert.

1 recipe of your favor-
ite cupcake (18–24,
baked and cooled)
1 recipe vanilla
buttercream frosting
green food coloring
plastic sandwich bag
green sprinkles or sugar

Place frosting and 2–3 drops food coloring in bowl and mix well. Scoop several spoonfuls of frosting inside bag. Squeeze all the air out and seal. Cut off bottom tip of plastic bag with a pair of scissors.

On the top of the cupcake, trace the shape of a 4-leaf clover with the frosting. Now, fill in the clover with the frosting. The clover will not cover every inch of the cupcake. Put desired amount of sprinkles on top.

New Year's Celebration

*With the special touch of sparkler candles, this cupcake
makes any party sizzle!*

---

1 box confetti cake
    mix
3 eggs
1 cup milk
1 tsp. vanilla
1 recipe vanilla
    buttercream frosting
sprinkles
sparkler candles

Mix together cake mix, eggs, milk, and vanilla. Pour batter into paper liners and fill ¾ full.

Bake at 350 degrees for 15–18 minutes or until cake springs back when lightly touched. Allow cupcakes to cool completely.

In a separate bowl, combine sprinkles and buttercream frosting. Frost cupcakes generously and place a sparkler candle on top. Light candles just before serving.

Picnic Cake
in a Jar

Picnic Cake in a Jar

This recipe is fun and different. Besides having your own glass to eat out of, it's creative and great to transport on a picnic or camping trip.

1 recipe of your favorite cupcake (batter only, not baked yet!)
6 (1 pint) canning jars
butter
6 canning jar lids and rims in boiling water
cookie sheet

Butter each jar well, being careful not to get anything on the rims. Pour 1 cup batter into jars, wiping off the top if spills occur.

Place jars evenly on a cookie sheet and bake at 350 degrees for 30–35 minutes. Remove from oven.

Using a hot pad or towel to protect your hands, immediately place the hot rim and lid on the pint jar, sealing tightly. Turn upside down and rest on a towel. Repeat with remaining jars.

Allow to cool and seal.

Frost with fruit or chocolate ganache. These cakes will keep in the refrigerator unopened for up to 3 weeks.

Pumpkin

Celebrate the harvest season with this festive cupcake.

1 recipe of your favorite
   cupcake (18–24, baked
   and cooled)
1 recipe chocolate
   buttercream frosting
red and yellow food coloring
candy corn
black gel icing
green gel icing

In a large mixing bowl, add 3–4 drops yellow food coloring and 1–2 red to get the desired color of orange you want.

Frost cupcakes with orange icing. Draw lines for grooves of the pumpkin with black icing. Place candy corn for eyes, mouth, and nose. Be creative! Use green gel icing to make a small stem at the top of the pumpkin if you desire.

Rainbow

At the end of every storm, there is always a rainbow somewhere.

- 2 recipes of your favorite cupcake (36–48, baked and cooled)
- 2 recipes vanilla buttercream frosting
- red, yellow, green, and blue food coloring
- 6 small bowls
- large platter (upside down cookie sheet works really well) for cupcakes to be decorated and presented on

Put 1 cup frosting into each bowl. Leave the remaining frosting in the mixing bowl. Add 3–5 drops of red food coloring into the mixing bowl and combine. Add blue food coloring to one smaller bowl, yellow food coloring to another, and green to another small bowl. Leave one bowl with white or plain frosting to top the "cloud" cupcakes.

Frost 14 cupcakes with red frosting and place in a half circle on the serving platter. Frost 11 cupcakes with yellow frosting and place them in a row, following the outline of the red. Frost 9 green cupcakes and repeat the placement next to the yellow. Then follow with 6 of the blue.

Frost remaining cupcakes with white frosting and place on either end of the rainbow, making them look like clouds.

Spring Garden

This is a great display of cupcakes for any spring birthday or shower. You can use this arrangement for your centerpiece, or as individual place settings for nametags. Your friends' faces will light up if you bring several on a plate to say "thanks" or "you're great!"

- 1 recipe of your favorite cupcake (18–24, baked and cooled)
- 1 recipe chocolate buttercream frosting
- 10–12 chocolate sandwich cookies, crushed into fine crumbs
- 1 box toothpicks
- 1 (16-oz.) bag gummy worms
- 1–2 (16-oz.) bags gumdrops

Frost cooled cupcakes with chocolate frosting and top with cookie crumbs. This is your "dirt."

Spear 24 gumdrops with toothpicks, using the bottom of the toothpicks to place into the cupcakes to secure. Set aside.

Break several toothpicks in half to make anchors for your flower petals. Cut the rest of the gumdrops in half, making the shape of a flower petal. Spear a halved gumdrop, securing with the toothpick and leaving space to secure to flower. Repeat until all petals have been secured.

To assemble the flowers, place the halved gumdrops around the center of the whole gumdrop. Place the long toothpick into the cupcake "dirt." Place 1–3 flowers on each cupcake. Place a gummy worm if desired at the bottom of the dirt.

The Icing on the Little Cakes

Caramel Cream
Chocolate Buttercream
Chocolate Ganache
Chocolate Mousse
Chocolate Sour Cream
Cream Cheese
Lemon Cream
Orange Cream Cheese

Peanut Butter
Pink Lemonade Cream
Root Beer Buttercream
Vanilla Buttercream
Whipped Cream
White Chocolate Mint
White Chocolate Mousse

Caramel Cream

Holy cow! Caramel cream tastes great on any of the chocolate cupcakes too.

- 4 Tbsp. butter
- ¼ cup brown sugar
- ¼ cup dark brown sugar
- 2–3 Tbsp. whole milk
- 1 cup powdered sugar
- 1 tsp. vanilla extract

Place butter and brown sugars in a medium skillet over medium heat. Stir and cook the mixture until it comes to a boil.

Add milk and bring the mixture back to a boil, stirring constantly.

Remove pan from heat and add powdered sugar and vanilla. Beat mixture with a wooden spoon until smooth and creamy.

Allow the cupcakes to cool slightly before frosting. Frosting will harden when cooled completely.

Chocolate Buttercream

Rich, chocolaty, and smooth—this frosting is a classic!

8 Tbsp. (1 stick) butter, room temperature

⅓ cup cocoa

3¾ cups powdered sugar, sifted

3–4 Tbsp. milk or cream

2 tsp. vanilla extract

Beat butter in a large mixing bowl until light and fluffy, about 30 seconds. Stop mixer before adding cocoa to avoid a large mess.

Add cocoa, sugar, 3 tablespoons milk or cream, and vanilla extract. Beat frosting starting on slow speed and add up to 1 more tablespoon milk or cream if frosting is too thick.

Chocolate Ganache

Ganache. Just that word makes you think, "It's too difficult and time-consuming. How can I ever do this?" But, if you just try it once, you'll be hooked. It's the best way to impress.

1 cup heavy whipping cream

12 ounces semi–sweet chocolate chunks or chips

Heat cream in a saucepan until it comes to a boil.

Remove from heat and pour over chocolate in a mixing bowl. Stir to mix together. You can pour it over your cakes warm, or allow to cool slightly and be spread like frosting.

Chocolate Mousse

This frosting is light, but rich in flavor.

---

1 recipe whipped cream

1 box (4-oz) chocolate pudding (powder only)

Add cream to large mixing bowl and pour pudding powder on top. Fold chocolate gently into the cream, without losing air from beaten cream.

Frost only completely cooled cakes. Keep refrigerated.

Chocolate Sour Cream

Deep, rich chocolate with a tangy zip adds depth and dimension to any choice of cupcakes.

- 8 Tbsp. (1 stick) butter, room temperature
- 3¾ cups powdered sugar, sifted
- 3–4 Tbsp. sour cream
- ¼ cup cocoa

Place butter in large mixing bowl. Beat until light and fluffy, about 30 seconds. Stop the mixer before adding sugar to avoid a large mess.

Add sugar and 3 tablespoons sour cream. Beat frosting starting on low, increasing your speed until frosting is nice and creamy. If the frosting is too thick, add 1 more tablespoon of sour cream, mixing thoroughly.

Cream Cheese

Sophisticated taste, and an even better look. This frosting is glossy and smooth.

8 ounces cream cheese, softened

½ cup butter, softened

3¾ cups powdered sugar

1 tsp. vanilla extract

Beat cream cheese and butter until smooth and light.

Stop mixer and add sugar and vanilla.

Start mixer on low and gradually increase the speed until frosting is fluffy.

Frost and refrigerate.

Lemon Cream

Lemons and cream. Did I say I have a favorite? Well, I should be honest—
every cupcake is pretty much my favorite.

- 2 cups heavy whipping cream
- ¼–½ cup powdered sugar (depending on preference)
- 1–2 tsp. lemon extract
- 1 Tbsp. grated lemon zest, finely chopped

Pour cream into large mixing bowl and begin to mix at low speed. Gradually increase speed until cream thickens and soft peaks form.

Turn off mixer and add sugar, lemon extract, and lemon zest. Start slowly again—no messes today!

Beat until stiff peaks form.

The stiffer the cream, the easier it is to frost the cupcakes. Keep refrigerated.

Orange Cream Cheese

Zesty and creamy are some of the best toppings to the perfect soft cupcake.

8 ounces cream
  cheese, softened

½ cup butter, softened

3¾ cups powdered
  sugar

1 tsp. orange extract

¼ cup frozen orange
  concentrate

Beat cream cheese and butter until smooth and light. Stop mixer and add sugar, orange extract, and orange concentrate. Start mixer on slow and gradually increase the speed until frosting is fluffy.

Frost and refrigerate.

Peanut Butter

This frosting is my son's favorite. He said, "I would put this on anything, even pancakes!"

1 cup peanut butter (chunky or smooth—
I prefer smooth)

½ cup butter, room temperature

2 cups powdered sugar

3–4 Tbsp. milk or cream

1 tsp. vanilla extract

Combine peanut butter and butter in a large bowl, mixing together until light and fluffy. Stop mixer before adding sugar.

Add sugar, 3 tablespoons milk or cream, and vanilla. Start slow and mix together, gradually increasing the speed. Mix until smooth and creamy. Add 1 tablespoon milk or cream if frosting is too thick.

Pink Lemonade Cream

Yummy! This frosting is sweet and tangy.

- 8 Tbsp. (1 stick) butter, room temperature
- 3¾ cups powdered sugar, sifted
- 3–4 Tbsp. milk or cream
- 1–2 drops red food coloring
- 2 tsp. lemon extract

Place butter in a large mixing bowl. Beat until light and fluffy, about 30 seconds. Stop the mixer before adding the sugar to avoid a large mess.

Add sugar, 3 tablespoons milk or cream, food coloring, and lemon extract. Beat frosting starting on slow speed and increasing your speed until frosting is nice and creamy. Add up to 1 more tablespoon of milk or cream if frosting is too thick.

Root Beer Buttercream

*I couldn't make a root beer cupcake and not
have root beer frosting to pair it with.*

- 8 Tbsp. (1 stick) butter, room temperature
- 3¾ cups powdered sugar, sifted
- 3–4 Tbsp. milk or cream
- 1 tsp. root beer flavoring

Place butter in a large mixing bowl. Beat until light and fluffy, about 30 seconds. Stop the mixer before adding sugar to avoid a large mess.

Add sugar, 3 tablespoons milk or cream, and root beer flavoring. Beat frosting, starting on slow and increasing your speed until frosting is nice and creamy. Add up to 1 more tablespoon of milk or cream if frosting is too thick.

Vanilla Buttercream

*A classic base to so many different recipes, this frosting will become
a favorite staple to your baking.*

- 8 Tbsp. (1 stick) butter, room temperature
- 3¾ cups powdered sugar, sifted
- 3–4 Tbsp. milk or cream
- 2 tsp. vanilla extract

Place butter in a large mixing bowl. Beat until light and fluffy, about 30 seconds. Stop beating before adding sugar to avoid a large mess.

Add sugar, 3 tablespoons milk or cream, and vanilla extract. Beat frosting starting on slow, increasing your speed until frosting is nice and creamy. Add up to 1 more tablespoon milk or cream if frosting is too thick.

Whipped Cream

You can choose stiff or loose peaks, depending on your preference. Stiff peaks are easier to frost and stand tall to make designs.

2 cups heavy
   whipping cream
¼–½ cup powdered sugar
   (depending on
   preference)

Pour cream into large mixing bowl and start mixing at low speed. Gradually increase speed until cream thickens and soft peaks form.

Turn off mixer and add sugar. Start slowly again—no messes today! Beat until stiff peaks form.

The stiffer the cream, the easier it is to frost the cupcakes. Keep refrigerated.

White Chocolate Mint

The white chocolate chunks are a great addition to this frosting.
The texture is outstanding.

- 8 Tbsp. (1 stick) butter, room temperature
- 3¾ cups powdered sugar, sifted
- 3–4 Tbsp. milk or cream
- 1 tsp. mint extract
- 1 cup finely chopped white chocolate

Place butter in a large mixing bowl. Beat until light and fluffy, about 30 seconds. Stop mixer before adding sugar to avoid a large mess.

Add sugar, 3 tablespoons milk or cream, and mint extract. Beat frosting starting on low, increasing your speed until frosting is nice and creamy. Add 1 cup finely chopped white chocolate into frosting. Add up to 1 more tablespoon of milk or cream if frosting is too thick.

White Chocolate Mousse

Soft and light with a hint of white chocolate flavor has made this frosting a favorite of my family.

- 1 recipe whipped cream
- 1 cup white chocolate chunks, melted and cooled

Add cream to large mixing bowl. Fold chocolate gently into cream, without losing air from beaten cream.

Frost only completely cooled cakes. Keep refrigerated.

Index

S

Slippery Butterfingers, 70
Sour Cream Blueberry, 24
Sour Cream Chocolate, 71
Spring Garden, 123
Strawberry Cheesecake, 25
Strawberry Shortcake, 27

T

Tutti Frutti, 28

V

Vanilla Buttercream Frosting, 137
Vanilla Pudding Poppy Seed, 29

W

Whipped Cream, 138
White Chocolate Mint Frosting, 139
White Chocolate Mousse Frosting, 140
White Chocolate Strawberry, 30
White Chocolate Vanilla, 72

Y

Yogurt Parfait, 31

About the Author

Wendy L. Paul has been cooking and baking for many years. She enjoys writing recipes and creating easy-to-make dinners and desserts. She and her husband, Brian, are the parents of three children, and oddly enough have a dog named Cupcake.

About the Photographer

Marielle Hayes is a photographer based in the San Francisco Bay Area. When she is not behind the camera, she enjoys traveling and spending time with her friends and family. She resides in the Oakland Hills with her husband, daughter, and Boston Terrier dog.